A Time to Laugh

A funny thing happened on the way to mission...

Peter Butt
and Others

ISBN: 9798876509772

"A time to weep, and a time to laugh; a time to mourn, and a time to dance..."

Ecclesiastes 3:4

PETER BUTT

Dedication

To everyone who has experienced the "joys" of mission.

To everyone who has enjoyed the privilege of travelling for the King and His Kingdom.

To everyone who can identify with the stories in this book.

Acknowledgements

Ken Ford, John Noble, Paul Randerson, Roger Blackmore and Ian Jennings – for your contributions:

Thank You!

Contents

Introduction

While enjoying a meal with my family some months ago, I shared one of the many unusual and somewhat amusing experiences of our 25 years travelling around the world. My daughter suggested that they should be written down, that it would be a shame if they were not recorded somewhere. I had completed four books and thought in my mid-70's that my days of writing had come to an end. However, the idea grew on me, and I realised that not only did I have some stories to share but I had many friends who had also experienced some amusing times on the road for Jesus.

I also saw this as a way of raising money for missions. We have produced this volume ourselves and paid for its publication. Every penny or pound raised from its sales will be given to mission.

Life has been very tough for many over these last few years.... Maybe as you read these accounts it will bring a smile to your face... After all, it is quite biblical, "there is a time to laugh".

Peter Butt 2024

Preface

Word is that the best ideas are the simplest ones that had merely never been thought of before. This book is an example of that, so full marks to Peter Butt and his friends for coming up with the concept of collecting some of the funny stories we all tell from time to time and putting them all together in one place, *A Time To Laugh*.

Peter and I have enjoyed a close friendship for over half a century now, and whether it was during the Bible College days of the late 60's, subsequent ministry ventures together at home or overseas, family vacations on sundrenched beaches, or the Christmases that we shared in homes that seemed to be bulging with kids, one thing we've always been able to do is see the funny side of events. We've done a lot of things together and we've laughed a lot together too.

Sadly, somewhere along the line a lot of people seem to have picked up the idea that churches are austere, miserable places to be, and I must admit some of the individuals who frequent them have not done a great deal to improve that picture. But as you'll see from the pages of this book, the contributors have all found a lot of joy in their journeys. Some of the lighter moments are planned, while others are like the stories you'll read here.

I often tell visitors to our church that while we're dead serious about what we do, we have a lot of fun doing it. I'm good with that because David wrote in Psalm 16 - *You make known to me the path of life; you will fill me with joy in your presence, with eternal pleasures at your right hand.*

A number of years ago Demos Shakarian, the founder of the Full Gospel Businessmen's Fellowship penned an autobiography that he entitled *The Happiest People On Earth*. That's us, God's people. Sometimes intentionally and other times accidentally but thank God for the gift of laughter.

1

Lost in Translation

1. Lost in translation – Peter Butt

Over the years we have experienced some interesting and amusing incidents in the translation of the teaching. There are many but I recount just a few that brought a smile to my face.

Barry Graham who was from the East End of London and was proud of his heritage and accent, was teaching for School of Ministries in Orissa, probably one of the most obscure and basic places that we visit. He was speaking on "grace" immediately after lunch. The main diet in this rural situation was rice, rice with everything. Massive amounts of rice were prepared to feed the 100 or so leaders attending this programme. Barry asked the leaders a question which

1

was then translated by the local guy. He asked, "Who wants more grace?"

Following translation there was an overwhelming negative reply as they all replied, "No". He repeated the question twice hoping for a different answer, but the reply was always negative. He turned to Basil, our local director for SOM and commented, "These guys don't wany more grace". It soon transpired that the translator struggling with Barry's accent using the word "grace" had said, "Rice" instead of "grace". They had heard the words, "Do you want any more rice". Hence the confusion which was soon rectified.

On another occasion in Kampala, Uganda, I was invited to preach at a church in the suburbs led by Wilson. A missionary lady had accompanied me to this church having just returned from a home visit to the UK. She was from the Fareham church led by Graham and Diane Bower. She brought greetings to the congregation from them. She said, "I bring you greetings from Graham and Di from Fareham". At which point people began to look at one another with concern and some even began to cry as a sadness descended on the people. After a short while, someone corrected the translator who had said, "I bring you greeting from Graham, his wife has Died". You can imagine the relief when the correct interpretation was given.

My final contribution was at a leaders' conference in Nairobi, Kenya. We had gathered significant leaders from various parts of Kenya together for teaching and training. Accompanying me on that occasion was a friend from North Carolina, USA. They have a very strong accent. It is the place where they say, "How are y'all". He was speaking and said, "You need Olaf All". I looked up as I did not understand what he was saying. I suggested he repeat it as the leaders around me were also looking at one another with the question "What did he say". He said it again, "Olaf All". After about 3 or 4 repeats I suddenly fell in. He was saying "Olive Oil". I have smiled again and again over that and usually mention it when we meet our friend in the US.

2. Careful with the accent – Ken Ford

Working through a translator presents various challenges – how good is their English, can they cope with your accent, are they actually interpreting what you're saying (!) and occasionally, can you understand their English when they speak to you? The last one is probably the rarest, but I've certainly experienced a couple of examples.

I was in Renggam, a town in the centre of Malaysia (see another entry for other details of my visit.) I had been with a Chinese congregation for three nights, and on the final night there was a very positive, faith filled atmosphere and I felt to invite people to come forward if they needed healing.

First up was a very elderly gentleman in shorts and a vest, looking hesitant but willing to reach out to God. I asked the lady pastor, who was interpreting for me, to inquire as to the nature of his ailment. She had a brief conversation with him and informed me 'He has bad feet.'

Looking down I could see that he was barefoot, and his toes did look somewhat gnarled and a little bruised. So, I knelt down, laid my hands on his feet and began to cry out to God for a full restoration of any damage that had occurred. I was in full flow when the pastor tapped me on the shoulder and said: 'No, no – bad epileptic feet.' I looked at her quizzically. 'Epileptic feet' she repeated.

I'm deeply aware of the limitations of my medical knowledge and wondered what the symptoms of epilepsy of the feet were – presumably some sort of shaking or trembling. The pastor was looking a little agitated and said again, firmly, 'Epileptic feet!' The phrase went over and over in my mind – 'Epileptic feet, epileptic feet....' And then I got it – epileptic fit!' Trying to look calm and confident I rose from my knees and began to pray a more relevant and meaningful prayer.

I left for Kuala Lumpur the following morning, so I'm unable to share any news of our friend's state of health, but I'd love to feel that he's free of epilepsy and has healthy, beautiful feet as a bonus.

A slightly different incident occurred in Durban, South Africa. I was chatting with a church member about the way in which the impact of the gospel had progressed over the years. He had a strong accent, but I was coping OK.

He informed me that when the holocaust came to South Africa it was a very challenging time. My knowledge of World War 2 history is a bit thin, and I realised I was totally unaware that South Africa had in any way been affected by the holocaust. I determined in my heart that on returning home, and ahead of any future visits to South Africa, I would ensure that I was better informed.

However, my faith in myself was restored later that day, when during the evening meeting the person, I had been speaking to earlier prayed a powerful and uplifting prayer, finishing with 'I pray this in the name of the Father, Son and Holocaust!'

3. Fish and Chips – Ken Ford

I've always felt it's really helpful to use familiar illustrations or anec-dotes when sharing or preaching. Of course, it was an approach frequently used by Jesus – 'Consider the lilies,' 'Look at the birds of the air,' 'A Sower went forth to sow' and so on. On returning to places where I've previously spoken, I've been delighted to find people can often remember my illustrations, though sadly they can't always recollect the point behind the illustration!

An important lesson to learn is that on overseas trips to different cultures, the illustrations that worked beautifully back home may not be quite so fruitful – images that are familiar and meaningful in Southampton, Birmingham and Plymouth, may not be so immediately relevant in Delhi, Durban or Kuala Lumpur.

I was speaking at a large church in East Malaysia, formerly Borneo, and seeking to make the point that we are to represent Jesus well – we should be good 'advertisements' for our faith. The young guy interpreting seemed a little hesitant, but overall, he was doing a good job and it felt like the congregation was with me.

Then illustration time came. Thinking of this idea of representing our 'product' well I declared, 'Can you imagine a skinny fish and chip shop owner!' A moment of silence followed, and the interpreter turned to me with that 'What did you say?' look. I repeated myself and here and there in the congregation people started to whisper to each other. 'Can you imagine a skinny fish and chip shop owner!' I said with slightly less confidence.

Looking somewhat panic stricken the young interpreter turned to the leaders seated on the platform behind us. One of them stepped forward and began to explain to the interpreter what I was trying to convey. It was clear that the word 'skinny' was not one the interpreter was familiar with, and the British obsession with fish and chips and its impact on the waistline was outside his experience. Eventually he returned to the microphone and passed on the information he had just received, and this was met with smiles and nods around the gathering. We were back on track.

The point I was trying to make seemed to be bearing fruit and I ventured further with my illustrative approach, informing the congregation that I had recently replaced some of the double glazing at our house. O dear! The same moment's silence, the 'What did you say?' look and the muttering amongst the congregation, one or two of whom seemed to understand what I was talking about. Once more the leader stepped forward and with various hand gestures attempted to explain to the interpreter what double glazing was. The interpreter then, with the same hand gestures, explained to the congregation and many seemed fascinated or bemused by the idea of two layers of glass in a window – I realised on reflection that many of my audience didn't have glazing, let alone double glazing.

Thus, the message took rather longer than I had anticipated but I console myself that in the future any visiting preachers who refer to skinny fish and chip shop owners, or extol the virtues of double glazing, will find a receptive and well-informed congregation. I do, though, have a slight fear that a year or two down the track from my visit there were numerous conversations where a church member said: 'Do you remember that English preacher who talked about chip shops and two layers of glass?' to which the reply will come: 'Yes, I remember it very clearly. Can you remind me what the point was that he was trying to make?' Ah well, it keeps you humble.

4. Whoops! Excuse the language – John Noble

Gerald Coates supplied us with a wealth of stories which kept us smiling for years. I shared this one at his funeral which many folks remembered as they were in the meeting at the time. Gerald was in full swing as he was deeply concerned for London and was encouraging us to pray for this great city since he had received a vision from the Lord of the evil that was encompassing it. He went on to explain that he had seen this huge octopus with a stranglehold on the capital with its massive 'testicles' stretching out across the whole area. At this point he stopped in his tracks as people all over the hall were struggling to contain their laughter with some almost falling on the floor. He could not at all see the funny side of what he had said until one of us on the platform was able to control ourselves long enough to explain that an octopus has 'tentacles'!

The scripture tells that laughter is like medicine and certainly a lot of people went home feeling much better after that meeting!

Christine and I did over 15 years of ministry at Spring Harvest and apart from seminars and counselling we were often asked to speak in the main venues. In fact, Christine was the first woman to minister in a main meeting in 1984. One year I was invited to speak at the 'alternative' meeting with around 1000 people on the subject of 'Twentieth Century Sexuality'. I was quite nervous as I didn't want to skate round the serious issues surrounding the subject which were almost always ignored. After I was introduced, a quiet hush fell on the congregation as folk didn't know what to expect. So, I took the bull by the horns and launched straight in at the deep end.

"One thing for sure in this twentieth century if we Christian are to be real, is that we have to take the matter of masturbation in hand!

I had no idea what was so funny, but the atmosphere was broken as people fell about laughing as and even the platform party failed miserably trying to control themselves. After people picked themselves up and order was restored the ice was broken and the talk went down really well with many thanking me for being so honest.

5. We could be here all night! – Ken Ford

The challenges of working through a translator have been acknowledged several times in these pages. One issue of course is the impact that the need for translation has on the length of the message you are seeking to present – the punchy, 25-minute word that went down so well back home, now requires at least 50 minutes to do it justice. Imagine then the impact of the need to translate not once but twice!

My wife Heather and I were in Goa, south India, with a team from our local church in Bridgwater, teaching at the Bible school there. The daytime sessions were going OK as all the students had a good grasp of English. However, this was not the case at the outreach gathering on the second evening we were there. We met in a half-built dwelling on a housing development on the edge of town. The atmosphere was wonderful, the house filled with expectant people with others peering through the open window spaces and over the half-built walls.

I was fully expecting to speak through an interpreter, but I hadn't been warned that the first translator would hand over to another who would give a further interpretation into the dialect spoken by the itinerant workers who were involved in the construction – I think it's called Kannada. This was my first, and only, experience of double translating.

I launched into my word, seeking, as you need to do in these situations, to make my phrases long enough to have some content to them, but short enough for the interpreter to keep up. The first couple of minutes seemed to go OK – introducing myself, 'pleased to be here' and so on. Translator number two appeared to be doing a good job each time he followed number one. The problems developed when I began to express some more specific aspects of the message I was seeking to bring – the phrases had a little more detail and content to them.

In my modest experiences of working with translators I had developed an approach that seemed to work really well for me. I would speak out a phrase and then, while the translator was doing their stuff, I would smile, look around and make eye contact with some of the gathered crowd. I took note of the people who smiled back or seemed to be nodding at what I was saying and waited for the interpreter to go quiet. Suddenly I was faced with the challenges of short-term memory loss.

I happily smiled and looked around while the first translator was in action; he then handed over to the second translator, who occasionally had to ask translator number one to repeat what he had said, and by the time translator number two had finished I had completely forgotten what the point was I was trying to make! So, I had to ask number one to remind me where I'd got to so that I could carry on. And of course, there was the growing fear that not only had I forgotten what I was saying but a large proportion of the gathering had forgotten as well!

Then, of course, the time issue came forcefully into my mind. I had estimated my preach was about thirty minutes. Double that for one translation, sixty minutes, add another thirty for translation number two plus an allowance for number one translator to remind me what I had said, and the occasional need for translator number one to ask number two to remind him of what I had said since he had forgotten – well, there was a growing prospect of being there all night!!!!!

Isn't the Holy Spirit wonderful! I managed to quickly adapt my approach, cutting back on my content, using shorter phrases and reducing the gazing around and smiling routine, and thereby we seemed to be able to pick up the pace and speedily get to the end.

What was truly remarkable was that everyone stayed to the end, and when an invitation was given to come forward for prayer for healing, a considerable number of people responded, and we saw God do some wonderful things. The whole episode simply served to remind me of what I think I've learned over many years – very often God does what he wants to do, not because of us but in spite of us.

6. Spoonerisms – John Noble

When I was a youngster my dad, a Salvation Army officer, introduced me to spoonerisms after he, in prayer on one occasion, prayed for people to be, 'blessed in boul and sody', which I never forgot. As our kids were growing up, I often used to play around with remarks which, when they were young often confused them.

Even now, young Thomas my great grandson gets caught out when I tell him that mummy's car is in the 'par cark'. He insists that I am wrong and repeats 'car park' over and over. Then I say it correctly and he replies, 'No grandpa, it's 'par cark', which really frustrates him.

My friend Hugh Thompson tells a story which I found hard to believe, but why should we let the truth spoil a good story? Apparently, Hugh was due to speak at a lady's meeting in a rather up-market area. There was also to be a violin recital by Mrs Peabody. The lovely lady who was chairing the meeting, after singing a hymn, introduced

Hugh in her incredibly posh voice and everyone clapped to welcome Hugh. She went on to say, "Before Mr Thompson speaks to us, I am going to ask Mrs Playbody to pea on her violin." Most of the ladies seemed able to pretend nothing had happened but Hugh was eternally grateful that during the recital he had to blow his nose and bring himself under control before he got up to speak.

2

On The Road

1. Jamaica – Irene's first visit

I remember my wife, Irene's first trip to Jamaica for all the wrong reasons. We were part of a team of 12 ministering across the island. We travelled together in a light blue transit van. It was an excellent visit with many memorable moments of Holy Spirit activity in the meetings and God breaking into many lives. However, there were two incidents where my wife unwittingly brought a moment of light relief by a couple of comments she made.

We were driving along a rural stretch of road; there were no houses or other buildings. In the distance we saw a man running. This was a regular occurrence in those days when people with mental health problems would be found just running and running along the road in various stages of undress. As we approached from the rear, the topic of conversation was around whether this man was completely naked or had some form of shorts on. We drove by still uncertain. However, Irene was the only one curious enough to look back, and blurted out, "Oh yes he is naked". The van was filled with laughter and my wife blushed as she realised what she had done.

On another occasion, Mike and Beryl Godward and Irene and I were in a car being driven by Leaford Kinkead. We were driving through Montego Bay and at the side of the road were several small stalls, many of them bicycles with a large container at the front, they were selling various food stuffs. One of them declared that for a small sum of Jamaican dollars you could enjoy "Cow cock soup". Having never heard of this I enquired of our Jamaican driver friend, "What on earth is cow cock soup". He was quite embarrassed and finding it difficult to reply until he eventually told us it was soup made from cow's testicles. My wife hearing this fascinating news declared, "Cows don't have cocks, it should be called Bullcock (ball cock) soup". This brought a response from all of us in the car. Mike seated in the front had a particularly loud laugh and for the next number of miles was beside himself with regular outbreaks of giggling. Fortunately, these were the only two comments of this nature made by my wife who is usually the epitome of discretion.

2. India by train – Jhansi, India to Cape Town, South Africa

Travelling in the developing nations can be interesting. Most of us who travel regularly have stories to tell of nightmare proportions. With cancelled flights, late arrivals, lost luggage, and many other experiences. My longest journey was from India to South Africa some years ago. I started the journey on Wednesday lunchtime and arrived in Cape Town on Saturday evening at 5pm to preach on the Sunday morning.

We had completed School of Ministries teaching sessions with some 100 leaders in Jhansi and were leaving on the lunch-time train to Mumbai, some 20 hours train journey across India. The train was about 3 hours late in arriving, so we spent that time on the steaming hot station waiting. The three of us settled into our carriage. It was a first class, airconditioned sleeping apartment for 4. Basil took the top bunk above me, Benny the top bunk on the other side of the carriage and an older gentleman joined us and took the other bed. There was only a curtain between us and the passageway so everyone who passed by made a noise of some kind and rustled the curtain.

As the evening approached, we settled down to sleep. The beds were very narrow, there was no place for our suitcases except under the bed and nowhere to put our belongings. I find it very difficult to sleep fully clothed, so I removed my shoes and socks, took off my trousers and found spaces to put them. I had a small net bag on the side of the bed in which I was able to put my glasses. I had a small dental plate at that time and could not find anywhere to place it, so I put it in one of my shoes, not the most hygienic solution.

The older gentlemen rapidly went off to sleep, snoring loudly and every now and again clearing his throat in a most irritating way. This did not help with sleep for the rest of us. Eventually we went to sleep expecting the journey to arrive at least 3 hours later than originally planned. I was awakened by Basil rushing into the carriage saying, quick we have arrived at our destination, get up, get dressed before the train leaves the station. Benny sat up totally dis-oriented shouting, "What's going on, what's happening?" Basil calmed him down and said to me, "You gather your things and I will take your case." I do not come round quickly in the morning at the best of times. I was sitting on the bed thinking through what I needed to do next, also aware that the first thing I usually did when I woke up was visit the bathroom. I found my glasses, put on my trousers, and reached down for my shoes. I had forgotten I had put my dental plate in the shoes and my feet connected with this object. I immediately cried out thinking that a mouse, rat or spider had entered my shoe. Of course, it was my teeth!

Basil came in at that time and laughed loudly at my predicament as he encouraged me to hurry along. I picked up my shoes and socks and left the compartment. My feet were bare, my shoes and socks in my hand, my hair which tends to be all over the place when I wake up was a mess. I left the train through the door to a sea of

Indian faces. Hundreds if not thousands of people were lined up on the platform. It felt as though every eye was turned to me. I was obviously a sight to behold. I doubt that any of those watching had ever seen an Englishman in such a state of disarray. I found a seat and put my socks and shoes on, then turned to Basil to inquire where the toilets were. He replied only on the train, which had not yet left the station. I returned to the train, managed the necessary, holding my breath in case I had to leap off the train at the last moment.

I spent two hours at Basil's home packing my case then we left for the Mumbai airport, a 2-hour drive. The flight to Dubai left on time and I arrived to spend some hours in the middle of the night in the airport. We left for Johannesburg the next morning where I met up with Irene, my wife, who had flown from London. We spent a couple of hours in the airport catching up before the final leg of the journey to Cape, where we arrived absolutely exhausted but grateful to God that we had made it!

3. Miami Vice

There have been several times in my travels when I felt somewhat vulnerable, even a little frightened. One of those times was not in darkest Africa or Asia but in the USA. I was on my way to Jamaica and passing through Miami. A leader I had met at a Conference had requested I stop in Miami for a few days, and he would arrange some meetings for me. I was uncertain about this, but he persisted and promised to look after me. I then made my travel arrangements to arrive on a Wednesday and stay through until the Sunday when I would fly on to Jamaica.

I arrived on time in Miami and waited to be collected from the airport by my friend, Miguel. After two hours of waiting, I decided to call the only telephone number I had and was answered by a lady who only spoke Spanish. She did not understand me at all. After spending all the coins n my possession, the only information I acquired was that Miguel was in Chile. So here I am in the airport knowing nobody and not having any idea what to do for the next few days. After another hour a guy turned up who I knew from a previous visit to Miami. His name was Lou, he was originally from Cuba. He said Miguel had requested he pick me up from the airport. We put my cases in the car, and he turned to me and said, "Where are we going then?" I said I have no idea, Miguel told me he had made all the arrangements. Lou replied, "The only thing I know is that you are preaching for the Elim church on Sunday, where are you staying?" After telling him I had no idea, he suggested I could stay with him and his wife Martha, they were now running a drug rehabilitation centre for ex-prisoners in an area called, "Little Haiti". Having no other option, I agreed. We arrived at a broken-down, narrow, poorly constructed, one-story building. We went in through the porch which was directly on the pavement.

This led to a narrow lounge/diner and into a small kitchen. There was one room off to the right which was Lou and Martha's bedroom and contained the only toilet in the place. Outside the back door was a shed/garage that housed 8 residents in bunk beds. That was the extent of the facilities. After a basic meal I was asked to share with these guys. They all looked to me as though they were still on some illegal substance. They glared at me as I sought to share the message of the love of Jesus.

There was a question in my mind. Lou had said they had a sofa bed that I could sleep on. I could not see it and wondered where I be spending the night. After a basic supper the residents went to their shed and Lou showed me where I would be sleeping. In the porch, which was totally glass there was a sofa that folded down into a bed. The problem was that if you put the bed down you could not open the door or put your case anywhere as the bed completely filled the room. Eventually I negotiated this problem and settled down to sleep. There were several broken panes of glass, and the wind blew through them and rattled the broken venetian blinds that were inadequately covering them. There was also the noise of shouting and screaming, of police sirens and even gun shots. I guess it was called "Little Haiti" for a reason.

I could not get to sleep and found myself praying. I did feel the Lord speak to me and suggest I felt vulnerable because I was travelling on my own and in the New Testament those on mission were instructed to go, "two by two". I determined never to travel alone again. I then needed to visit the bathroom. I put it off as long as possible but had to get up. To open the door, I had to close the sofa bed, open the front door of the property and visit the toilet in the bedroom where Lou and Martha were sleeping. I closed the bed, opened the door and in the darkness trod on the dog who was sleeping in the doorway. He barked loudly and a guy, who I did not realise was sleeping on the sofa sat up, frightening the life out of me and general chaos ensued. It was like something from a comedy show. I then knocked on the door of Lou's bedroom to request permission to use the loo. Having negotiated that, I spent the rest of the night working out what to do between now and Sunday. I could not spend another night in this place.

I planned to visit friends in Melbourne Beach some 200 miles up the coast. I called them and made the arrangements, bought a ticket for a greyhound coach, and arrived the next afternoon. I had Thursday and Friday with them and arranged to travel back on the Saturday for the preaching engagement on the Sunday.

On the coach returning to Miami, I rehearsed my speech for Lou. I would request he take me to a hotel as I needed to sleep and prepare for the Sunday meeting without any distraction. Lou was waiting for me, and I shared my thoughts. He said, "There is no need to do that, I have an office in the town, and it has a bed as I sometimes sleep over. We arrived at the office which was over a strip of small shops. He suggested we visit the Coffee shop first. It was a Cuban establishment. We entered and sat down. There were about 20/30 people in the place. Within seconds of us sitting down, a fight broke out between two of guys, within minutes everyone else joined in. It was like watching a Western film. They were breaking tables and hitting one another with chairs. We were just sat there. I said to Lou that perhaps we ought to leave. As we did several police cars turned up and started hauling the pugilists away. We went to another coffee shop and Lou began to sweat profusely. I asked if he was OK, and he then told me he had Aids and that before he came to the Lord, he was leading a different kind of life and had contracted this life-threatening disease. I spent some time ministering to him before we went up to the office. It was part of several offices that shared the same facilities.

The office itself was fairly spacious and there was a sofa bed at one end which had seen better days. As he left he mentioned to me that according to his contract you were not really supposed to sleep in these offices so I could not leave the room during the night. If I need the loo, I should use the wastepaper bin in the corner and I should not go to the bathroom until 9am in the morning. So now I am breaking the law! I settled down to sleep and the phone in the office rang about 1pm in the morning. There was someone rattling away in Spanish, Lou was running a kind of advice centre. I tried to explain but put the phone down only for it to ring again a few minutes later with someone else on the end of the line. I took the plug out of the phone and managed a couple of hours sleep. I crept down to the washroom and did the necessary before Lou came to pick me up for the meeting. I did not feel like preaching, I was tired, fed up and looking forward to leaving Miami.

The church had several hundred people attending. Mike Wittman, the leader was very welcoming. Following the worship, I preached. I do not know if I have ever had a greater sense of anointing. As I spoke, I began to prophesy to this one and that. The meeting started at 10am, I prophesied over so many people I lost count. It was 2pm when I finally sat down. It was one of the most remarkable experiences of my life. Maybe it was because I was so dependent on the Lord, I had nothing to give after my experiences. I am not sure I would want to go through that again!

4. Cruising down the Amazon River – Paul Randerson

We had been travelling all day, down the Amazon River on a boat, in stinking, tiring heat. I preached that evening in 42 degrees heat. After the meeting I finally dropped into a hammock on the pastor's porch exhausted. As I settled down, I realised I needed to pass water. I looked under the hammock to extract myself safely and discovered that the pastor's son's puppy had pooped all over the floor under my hammock. Yes...You guessed it. The journey to relieve myself was accompanied by me having to manoeuvre the sticky mess. It was a real slipslop.

One of the hazards of such travel is stomach problems. On one occasion I had terrible stomach upset which had lasted for 48 hours. I was on the platform waiting to preach when my stomach began to speak to me. It said, "When you got to go you got to go". I told my interpreter I urgently needed the toilet. He told the pastor leading the meeting. I was led by a deacon to a dark wooden hut behind the wooden church. As we opened the creaking door, a million large blue bottle flies exited. I noted it was a dreaded long drop. The deacon closed the door. I put my torch in my mouth, removed my trousers and underwear, wrapping them round my neck. At that moment my evacuation which was supposed to go down the long drop decided to go in another direction completely and shot all the way up the back wall. After cleaning up as best as I could, I told my interpreter who then told the pastor, who called two deacons to go clear up the toilet. It brought a whole new understanding of the deacon's role in that church in the Amazon.

After a long morning travelling and meeting with jungle leaders, I was offered a shower. A 40-gallon drum filled with water, dispensed the liquid from overhead. A small three walled area with a door made up the shower room but it was in complete darkness.

I felt something moving by my feet as I showered so I opened the door slightly to see what it was and was surprised to see a large turtle.

After the meeting in the evening, we went back to pastor's jungle hut. We were served a large bowl of something fishy and rubbery; it was the turtle; I was eating my shower mate.

The joys of travel in the Amazon.

3

Chaotic Meetings

1. Ashford, Invaded by an enemy – Peter Butt

Following Bible College four of us who had become particular friends, arranged to spend a week's holiday on the Kent coast. This was a year after we had graduated. Along with our partners and our newly born baby we spent the week in two caravans; enjoying catching up and sharing our aspirations for the future. I guess we all secretly believed we were the answer to the spiritual malaise in Britain and we were like young Billy Grahams awaiting recognition. There was perhaps a little arrogance in us as young men and women in our early to mid-20's.

On the Sunday as good Pentecostals we made our way to a "Gospel Meeting". We had to travel a few miles and had difficulty in locating the meeting place which turned out to be a quite a small room which would have struggled to hold more than 30 people.

When we arrived, the meeting was about to commence, and we trundled in and filled the back row of the small room. We doubled the size of the congregation. Not only that but everyone else except the Pastor's daughter were more than double our age. She was probably in her 30's and sat ln the front row next to her mother.

The Pastor beamed with joy as he thought revival had come. He was a very pleasant man, quite short and a little stout; he also wore a dog collar. He reminded me of the kind of church leaders that appear in cowboy films from the Wild West of the 19th century. He led the meeting with gusto, even finding room to have a little dance, very unusual in the early 70's.

He began to preach and was well into his subject when a demonic invader interrupted the gathering. Flying from side to side of the room a wasp entered the meeting. The eyes of everyone in the congregation instead of being fixed on the preacher and the words that came from his mouth, watched the antics of this foreign beast. It was like watching a game of tennis at Wimbledon. Eyes went to and fro in tune with this intruder.

I mentioned the Pastor's daughter, she was seated on the front row and as all good Pentecostal ladies of that era was wearing a hat! It was a solid red colour and firmly planted on her head. After entertaining us for what seemed an age the wasp decided to settle on her hat. The older gentleman seated in the row immediately behind her felt he had to deal with this menace. He raised his red, hard back "Redemption Hymnal" and crashed it down on the unsuspecting lady's hat. She nearly fell off her chair. The noise interrupted the preacher's flow and 8 recently graduated Bible College students burst into uncontrollable laughter. For the rest of the meeting, we hardly dared to look at each other as we were struggling to contain our equilibrium. Our supper time that evening consisted of retelling the story over and over and enjoying the experience again and again.

We did hear several years later that this church did grow and purchased their own building.

2. Baptisms in Barnet

I had been leading the church in Barnet for 3 years. It had been hard graft picking up a very small congregation and at last seeing signs of growth. On our third anniversary our friend Roger travelled down from his church in Sheffield to be our guest speaker. We also took the opportunity to hold our first baptismal service. We had 3 people signed up to be baptised.

It was the last weekend in October so not that warm. In fact, it was pretty cool for that time of the year. An old lady of 89 had spoken to me the week before and indicated her desire to be baptised but had expressed her reticence because of her fear of catching cold. She had a displaced kneecap so walked with difficulty. She was very short and very frail. One of our ladies standing nearby offered to bring a ladies swimming cap so she would not get her hair wet. She agreed to go ahead, and the cap was produced on the day.

In those days we used long white gowns for those who were being baptised. Our dear old lady had very white skin, the bathing cap appeared – it was white with the numbers 29 on the front. Our baptismal candidate looked very ghostly white in her uniform. Following the meeting and an excellent preach from Roger the Baptismal part of the gathering began.

There had been an "immersion water heater" in the tank for 24 hours but as we walked down the steps the coldness of the water attacked us with ferocity. We decided to baptise the old lady first. As was the custom she gave a short testimony of her faith in Jesus, we sang the baptismal song, "Follow, follow, I would follow Jesus......" As she was about to descend the stairs, I unable to resist, said to Roger, "Come in number 29 your time is up". (A little explanation is due here. In the 70's if you hired a rowing boat or some such vehicle it would be inscribed with a number. When it was time for you to return it, you would hear your number over the P.A. letting you know your time was up.) Roger immediately began to giggle, and I joined him, we were halfway through the song, I managed to start it again until we had regained control of ourselves. As the lady descended the steps, she let out a yelp as the freezing water touched her skin. We baptised her; I am not sure we actually put her fully under the water, but I am sure heaven was happy that she had taken this step. She did not have any adverse reactions and continued as part of the church.

The next candidate was a young lady completely unchurched; her own baptism was the first she had attended. She had on the standard white gown. Weights were meant to be put in the hem of the garment to keep it down when in the water. Unfortunately, this young lady had not been instructed with this information, so we had our work cut out to protect our young woman's dignity without causing any unhelpful public embarrassment. I am delighted to say we managed that well.

Overwhelmed by the occasion I then offered baptism to any in the congregation who had been challenged by those who had taken this step and would like to also be baptised.

There was an old man who attended the meeting, he was originally from Switzerland. I had visited him on a number of occasions. His wife and son attended the church, but he had fallen out with a church in another town years before he moved and was very caustic in his comments about the church. He stood up and requested that he be baptised. That was a great challenge to a 25-year-old young leader. No one had trained me or instructed me what to do in this situation. I had offered baptism to any who would like to follow Jesus in this way and this man who I did not believe was a follower of Jesus had requested we baptise him. I leapt out of the pool, leaving Roger to freeze, and accompanied our friend into the vestry which served as a men's changing room. My mind was racing, I was asking God for His help and totally out of my comfort zone. I asked him if he was a follower of Jesus. In an aggressive voice he answered, "Of course I am". He was a rather large gentleman and I suggested it would better to wait as we did not have any clothes to fit him. He replied he was wearing shorts. I was impressed, he had come prepared. I then had a moment of inspiration. I said that before I baptised him, I would ask him a series of questions after which I would baptise him. I thought I would ask him if he was a believer in Jesus, that he believed Jesus had died to save him from his sin, that he was determined to follow Jesus. I then baptised him on the "confession of His faith". I felt this exonerated me from responsibility of baptising an unbeliever.

To return to the event. He remained in the changing room to prepare himself and I returned to the freezing tank where Roger was shivering. After several minutes he came from the vestry wearing his underpants. His view of shorts and mine were a little different. I shot out of the pool and used myself as a shield to protect the people from this awful sight. We got through the questions, he was baptised. At

31

the end of the evening as we were leaving the chapel, we visited the vestry to find a large pair of underpants left in a pool of water in the middle of the floor. My wife washed and dried them and returned them to the gentlemen a couple of days later. He never came to any church meeting after that.

However, not long after that his health deteriorated, and he was taken into hospital. He rapidly declined and was in a coma. I went to visit him. He was to all intents and purposes unconscious. I held his hand and said to him. "If you know you are a believer in Jesus and are trusting Him for salvation and expect to live with Him for eternity, please squeeze my hand." He then squeezed my fingers; it was one of those Holy moments for me. He very soon afterwards died. I believe I will see him in heaven.

3. Ice Cream and Meetings – Peter Butt

I first met Menzie Oban in north London in the early 70's. He visited the church I pastored in Barnet. He made a great impression on me. He hailed from Jamaica and had come to England in the early 50's. He was a drug addict and was in a serious condition. He was witnessed to on the streets of London by Derek Prince and was extraordinarily transformed. He was returning to Kingston, Jamaica to set up a drug programme to encourage others to put their trust in Jesus and not get involved in an addictive lifestyle. When I visited

Jamaica in the mid-80's I met him again in Montego Bay where he was leading a Christian Centre which housed a church, a school, a trade school, and a conference centre. He was still an extraordinary man. He would regularly break into song, pray in the middle of the pavement surrounded by people, challenge people about their life and witness to the grace of God. He was only a small guy but absolutely fearless.

I once took a team to Jamaica, and he met us in the airport. It was crowded like a football stadium: there were 12 of us mainly young people. We were looking for our host when suddenly we heard a cry. Above the hubbub and noise of the crowd. "Brother Peter", the voice said. It was Menzie, we couldn't see him, but we could certainly hear him. He then broke into song. "Praise the Lord, Praise the Lord let the earth hear His voice". He sang right through the chorus as he made his way over to us. He gathered us into a scrum and began to pray, he could not do anything quietly, so the team, weary and tired from our long journey were in a state of shock as he thanked God for our safe arrival and prayed God's blessing upon us.

One incident that has stayed in my memory was on a visit where we were the main speakers at a conference. Following the meeting we went to the local ice-cream parlour. I believe it was called, "Friend-lies" It was an establishment from the USA and was around the Easter season. The local custom there is that at Easter Jamaicans would enjoy "bun and cheese". I believe there were approximately 10 of us.

We went to the counter and ordered our ice-creams after which we took our seats together in a corner of the large restaurant. We had hardly began to enjoy eating our delicious looking purchases when Menzie stood up and began to speak. His message went something like this. "You could not come to the meeting, so we are bringing the meeting to you. Easter is not about bun and cheese but about a man who gave his life to transform ours and forgive us for all the wrong we have committed. Let us pray". He then proceeded to request that the staff took their hats off as we were going to pray. They all concurred without any hesitation. He then prayed for everyone in the store that they would come into a relationship with Jesus. He concluded the prayer with the words, "If this establishment is righteous – bless it. If not close it down, Amen."

The team and I continued to keep our heads down and devour our ice-creams. Not quite knowing what had just happened.

When we returned to Montego Bay the next year. Friendlies had closed!

4. Kenley – Oxted

While at Bible College it was the practice for students to visit churches in the area each Sunday. If you required a lunch, you had to order it in an appropriate book. There were two headings: Name and Place. One of the students was visiting a church in a place called Harold Hill. The girl making the lunches gave him two meals thinking it was two people. I found that amusing...

As we came to the end of our college course my friend Roger and I realised we had never been out on ministry together on a Sunday. We sought to rectify this and requested we have a day together in ministry. We were appointed to visit a church in a Kent village called Oxted. We were collected at the College by one of the leaders of the church. He had an E-type Jaguar. We travelled in style and very swiftly to the church for the morning meeting. We negotiated the morning meeting a little "high" from our journey to the church. The guy and his wife owned a bakery. We were treated to a glorious dinner and stuffed ourselves with the finest food, the dessert I remember was outstanding. We then watched the Sunday football, it was on ITV called the "Big Match"; we played darts with the guy and had a generally relaxing afternoon before tea was served with delicious, mouth-watering cakes from the bakery. We felt like a snooze after this lazy, slovenly afternoon but found it was time for the evening "Gospel Meeting". Along we went fed up, watered, with full stomachs, not a lot of prayer and preparation and certainly not ready for the gathering.

I was leading the meeting and Roger was preaching. Students were also expected to produce a singing item. Neither Roger nor I saw this as our particular gift but we were prepared to give it a whirl. We chose the song "Burdens are lifted at Calvary". I handed the music over to the very accomplished young man at the piano and we proceeded with the song. We manoeuvred the first verse but at the end of the first line of the second verse Roger missed a word and my singing of the word "see" was followed a second later by his rendition. We were not in a very "spiritual state of mind" having spent the day indulging in various frivolous activities. This resulted in me giggling at Roger's mistake and him joining me. The pianist continued to play as Roger and I stood giggling on the platform in front of the congregation.

This state of affairs lasted the whole of the second verse and chorus and through into the third verse and chorus as well. We did try on one or two occasions to rectify the situation only to make it worse. One wonders what the congregation made of our fiasco. Maybe they would be surprised that we each have over 50 years of ministry and church leadership. I do remember the secretary of the church brought the notices immediately after we had concluded our song and apologised that we had not been able to complete our assignment. When laughter broke out in the church as a result of the refreshing in the mid-90's, uncontrollable laughing in church was not a new experience to Rog and me.

5. Gerald Coates Speechless – John Noble

I was invited by Peter Butt to minister at a "family week" in Sussex, organised at the end of 3 weeks of Youth Camp activity. I was to speak on the Wednesday evening and my friend Gerald Coates was to speak the next evening. Gerald was well known for his story telling and when he found a good one, he couldn't resist telling it everywhere he spoke. He would repeat it over and over until he found another.

On this occasion he had just returned from a trip to South Africa and everywhere he went he would tell the story so I knew he would use it to kick off with this group. So, I explained that I was going to tell his story and suggested when he mentioned the story about the cat, they should all call out we've already heard it. It was a good story about a cat, although probably not true.

A couple in the pastor's church where Gerald was staying, had bought a kitten as a present for their daughter. The mother and daughter went out and told the father that under no circumstances was he to let the cat out of the house. Within a few minutes of them leaving the father left the front door open, and the playful kitten climbed a thin tall tree in their garden and refused to come down. In the end he hatched a plan and threw a rope up the tree as far as possible. He then tied the rope to the bumper of their car with a view to pulling the tree down and rescuing the cat. the only problem was that the rope snapped, and the kitten went flying through the air, over the roof of a nearby house, never to be seen again!

The next day the pastor was in the local store and saw another member of the church buying cat food. He said to her that he had not realised she had a cat. She explained that she had not bought a cat, but she was in her garden seated at a picnic table with her small son who said to his mum he would like a kitten. He said at Sunday School last week the teacher said we could pray for whatever we want, and Jesus would give it to us. The mother suggested that perhaps it was not appropriate to pray for such things. However, he went ahead and asked Jesus for one. She explained with amazement that when he finished praying, they opened their eyes, and a kitten came flying through the air and landed on the table in front of them. Her son looked at her with a kind of smug smile on his face. She said she had never had such an immediate answer to prayer before in all her life and her son was delighted.

 I heard that when Gerald told the story everyone called out "We have heard it". He was quite thrown by this reaction, unusually for Gerald, for a moment he did not know what to say. After a few seconds as he realised what I had done, he said something like. "That rat John Noble, he told you". It was moment of great hilarity.

6. A near death experience – Ken Ford

Mealtimes can be one of the great delights of overseas trips, but you do need to be careful as the conversation develops.

I was with my buddy Pete Light in a certain nation – I'd better not say which one to avoid causing offense, though I do believe the delightful couple involved have both gone to glory. We were staying with the pastor and his wife and joined them at the Sunday morning church service.

It had become a tradition at the church that the pastor's wife would sing a solo at the morning meeting, and so our hostess came to the front to offer her contribution. One or two of the congregation looked a little uncomfortable, and we soon discovered why. Our beloved sister was undoubtedly a gifted woman who loved Jesus with a passion and was well endowed with enthusiasm and energy. Sadly, tuneful singing was not among the gifts which the Holy Spirit had released to her. I'm no musical expert but the key in which she was singing seemed to bear no resemblance to the key in which the musicians were playing – is there such a key as H sharp?

Fortunately, Pete and I were sitting alongside each other – had our eyes been able to meet I dread to think what emotion we might have displayed. We held ourselves together and by the grace of God managed to nod approvingly as the contribution drew to close. The meeting moved on and I recollect a good, uplifting time.

Following the service, we returned to the pastor's house where his wife served lunch for us – I'm glad to say her culinary skills were well up to standard and a hearty plate of rice with a tasty sauce was on my plate in front of me. While our soloist was in the kitchen we reflected on the morning's gathering, and the pastor, keen to honour his wife, mentioned a recent trip they had made to Singapore. In a clear, slightly emotional, and proud voice he announced: 'When my wife sang in Singapore, everyone cried.'

I had just taken a mouthful of rice. Unlike the church situation, Pete and I were facing each other, and our eyes met. Strange feelings started to rise up in me and I strongly doubted if I was going to be able to keep my emotions under control. However, I gritted my teeth firmly together and quietly prayed that the conversation would move on rapidly.

But no! Keeping his eyes on me, and aware of my mouthful of rice, Pete, in the calm, slow, droll and emotionless voice for which he is renowned, uttered the words: 'I can really understand that bro!'

To this day I cannot believe that my mouthful of rice failed to end up on the opposite wall of the dining area. My chest and throat froze solid, and my heart pounded as I fought to keep control, and our host did look at me with a somewhat inquisitive gaze. After a while I managed to pat my stomach with that 'Oh, a touch of indigestion I fear' look, and eventually my rice was able to descend rather than reappearing.

So do take my advice. In these situations, take small mouthfuls and swallow quickly lest the conversation raises potential mirth hazards.

7. Preachers Questions – Roger Blackmore

The fact that our church's mission is to reach the unchurched means that there is often a considerable number of people in our services with neither a background of churchgoing nor an understanding of normal church etiquette.

This point was brought home to me one Sunday morning some years ago, when my preaching was in full flow on the subject of prayer. I was attempting to point out that too often our prayers are little more than thinly veiled efforts at telling God how he should act in a given situation. I suggested that we should be asking for God's will to be done rather than pushing for what we think he should do.

And that was when I made the fatal mistake. In the moment, I was totally oblivious to the fact that there were people present who might not realize that when a preacher asks a question, chances are he's not looking for the answer, rather he is about to answer it himself.

So, I continued, at full throttle, "After all, what was your life like before you knew Christ and you were calling all the shots?"

As a booming voice shouted out an expletive from midway back that everyone could hear, the place collapsed into laughter, and I remembered that unchurched people do unusual things. Trust me, it took a few minutes to pull everyone back in and finish the sermon.

8. Animal Magic – Roger Blackmore

At one time we rented a pretty scruffy movie theatre for our Sunday services. It really wasn't great at all, but it was the only vaguely suitable building in that area. We had some good times there.

One Sunday morning as the band was leading worship, I picked up that the drummer wasn't playing and looked over to see what was happening. In the low lighting, it was very difficult to make out why there was this interruption, but I could see that the drummer was bending over and looking at something at his feet. Then he reached down with a drumstick and appeared to flick something up from the floor, that flew across the front of the stage and only just missed the bass player's face. And with that, the drums started up again.

Turns out, the bass pedal had suddenly jammed and when he looked down, the drummer realised he had just squashed a rat that was running underneath it. It was stuck there, so he figured he'd try to poke it out and in the process, ended up sending it airborne in the direction of his colleagues. We didn't stay in that theatre much longer!

4

Difficult Domestic Situations

1. Strangely Warmed – Ken Ford

In the steps of Wesley. The great challenge of overseas trips is adapting to the procedures of the culture in which you find yourself. Lack of awareness concerning minor procedural differences can have disturbing consequences.

On one occasion I found myself staying with a pastor and his family in a township outside Durban in South Africa. It was a delightful experience – I never discovered how many of the numerous children were his own and how many were needy youngsters he had taken in, but the atmosphere was relaxed and welcoming.

On my third afternoon, I was having a lie down, thinking through what I might share at the evening meeting. There was a gentle tap on the door and a young girl entered and announced 'Pastor, your bath is ready.' This was something of a surprise – I hadn't requested a bath, but after a few days travelling maybe my hosts had become aware of a need for me to freshen myself up. So I dutifully gathered by washing kit and followed her out.

The bathroom turned out to be a small shed attached to the rear of the house. There was a large boiler on the wall which dispensed boiling water into the tin bath below. There were a couple of buckets of cold water alongside which could be added to bring the water to the most comfortable temperature. My young companion bid me farewell and left me to enjoy a peaceful and relaxing soak.

I began to add cold water to the steaming hot bath and gradually brought it to an acceptable temperature, removing my clothing I climbed over the edge and lowered myself into the water.

In my school days I aways erred away from the scientific side of learning so issues of heat transference and temperature maintenance were not uppermost in my thinking. Unlike most people, it did not occur to me that a tin bath would retain the temperature of the boiling water long after the water itself had been cooled by the adding of cold water.

As I lowered myself to a seating position a somewhat disturbing feeling came over me. On May 24th, 1738, John Wesley was at a Moravian meeting in Aldersgate Street, London, listening to someone reading from Martin Luther's preface to the Epistle to the Philippians, and he famously said that he felt his heart 'strangely warmed.' I can confirm that I know exactly how he felt, although in my case a different part of my anatomy was involved! Further details would be inappropriate, but the bottom line is that at the meeting that evening I chose to remain standing for the entire duration of the worship, and the lengthy car journey the following day was something of an endurance test.

So, you have been warned – think before you sink, test before you rest and learn before you burn.

2. Washing in Jamaica and Uganda

Having been so used to having unlimited access to both water and electricity it does come as a stark reminder of our privileged lifestyle when visiting developing nations.

My first experience was on my first trip to Jamaica. This beautiful island with its rich culture and history overwhelmed me. We enjoyed our trip taking in the brilliant sunshine and also preaching and teaching in various churches and training situations around the island.

However, on one occasion I was a little out of sorts. We were staying in an excellent house on the outskirts of Montego Bay. The area was called Torado Heights and is known for its excellent housing and mansions. We were staying in a 10-bedroom house, each room with a balcony overlooking the private swimming pool. My en-suite bathroom was a blessing. One morning I was enjoying a shower, the water is very soft, and I had "soaped up" and was covered in lather when the flow of water suddenly stopped. It did not start again either. (I have since discovered that the water came from a well and was pumped up to the house by an electric pump, when the electricity was cut off, the water flow immediately ceased). What do you do.... I was covered in sticky, soapy water?

I had a meeting to speak at 30 minutes later. I scrapped off the lather the best I could with a towel and spent several hours feeling extremely uncomfortable. On returning to the house, thankfully the electricity was restored, and I was able to wash the remainder of the lotion from my body. I learnt a lesson. I decided that when in the future I was taking a shower in such unpredictable circumstances I would fill the basin with water before taking a shower, at least I could then wash the soap from my body!

Another time in Uganda it was even more horrific. I was leaving the church in Kampala in which I was ministering to travel to South Africa. My flight was leaving Entebbe airport at 7.30am. I made arrangements with the hosts to leave my room and put the key through the letter box when I left. I had arranged to be collected at 5.30am to arrive at the airport in time to board the aeroplane. I got up around 5am to have a shower before the journey. It was dark at this time. I again "soaped up" ready for the shower. This time not only did the power go down, but the lights went out as the water stopped flowing. A double disaster. I could not see at all. I was covered in soapy lather; I had not completed my packing. So again, I did the best I could with the help of a towel. I managed to put everything into my case with the help of a small torch.

At 5.30am I was ready to leave the room although dishevelled and very uncomfortable. I left the room, locked it with the key and put the key through the letter box. At that moment in the pitch darkness, it decided to rain, African style. There was nowhere to go or shelter from the torrent of rain. I dragged my cases to the front of the building and found a slight overhang over the roof which meant I was able to remain reasonably dry. I waited for my driver to pick me up. 20 minutes went by and there was no sign of him. When 6am came I was getting a little worried. I found his number and telephoned him. He took an age to respond and apologised profusely that he had forgotten and was still in bed. Some 15 minutes later he turned up. The day was not going well.

In driving rain, he managed to get to Entebbe in record time. I was rendered speechless by the journey. Driving at breakneck speeds, flying around corners in the pouring rain, I was amazed we were still alive. I thanked him, rushed into the airport expecting to be told I was too late for the flight. Thankfully it was slightly delayed, and I was able to get on board. I was so late that I took all my luggage with me on board, and they closed the door immediately I joined the flight. We had an uneventful journey to Johannesburg, South Africa.

Arriving in South Africa, which I had visited many times, I made my way to passport control. At the desk I was asked for my Yellow Fever Certificate. I said, "Yes I have one, but it is in my office back in the UK". I had visited SA many times and had never before been asked for a Yellow Fever certificate. It was explained to me that it was only required when you came into SA from another African country. I had always travelled directly to SA before, so it was not required. The good news was that there was a clinic available where I could complete this injection and be on my way. I entered the clinic to be told the cost would be US$40. I did not have that amount of dollars with me. The nurse suggested I went to the cashpoint. However, that was situated the other side of passport control and I was not allowed to access it. I prayed... then I prayed... I had a moment's inspiration.

I asked if I could pay with a number of currencies to reach the required sum. This was acceptable so I put together my Ugandan shillings, my British currency, the few US dollars I had, and a few South Africa Rand from a previous trip. I was still 1 US$ short. The nurse had mercy on me and completed the task of sticking the needle in my arm. This made me even more uncomfortable with the soap still irritating my skin. I then caught my next flight to Durban and was met and driven 70 miles to Pietermaritzburg. I was allowed to go to my room, had a quick shower and was then taken to a meeting where I was expected to speak. By the time I had completed my task it was quite late in the evening. I was so delighted when I was able to lay my head on the pillow and rest. What a day! I am sure it will make you smile but enduring it was not particularly enjoyable".

3. Life's great questions ‑ Kenford

In my modest experience there are two major questions that dominate one's thinking on any overseas trip. Firstly, what is God saying to this group of people he has given me the privilege of ministering to? Secondly, what is the current state of my bowels? Over various trips I would have to say that the latter question has often been of more immediate concern than the former.

I have often travelled with my friend Pete Light. Pete has a very caring and supportive nature, and being aware of my gastric challenges, at some point each day on our trips, in his unique and laid-back style, he would gently ask me 'Ere bro, ave you been?'

This became such a memorable part of our travels together that at a gathering to celebrate Pete's years in ministry I felt led to pen a song reflecting this aspect of our relationship. I guess this isn't an audio book you're perusing, so you're spared my vocal presentation, but here are the lyrics:

I've travelled many times with Pete, we know each other well,

We've prayed and preached and prophesied and stormed the gates of hell.

We've often sought the Lord to see what wisdom we can glean,

But it always comes back to life's great question, 'Ere bro, ave you been?'

The first trip we went on our Jumbo Jet was set to start,

We'd checked in late, so we were seated forty rows apart.

The captain's voice came out loud and clear: 'We'll be in Delhi at three fifteen.'

Then Pete's voice came out louder and clearer: 'Ere bro, ave you been?'

I well remember the first time Pete invited me to preach,

I sought the Lord and picked a well-known text from which to teach.

Pete stood at the back to encourage me as we turned to John 3 16,

As I'm about to start I see him mouthing: 'Ere bro, ave you been?'

There was one prophetic meeting I was feeling quite in need,

So I thought I'd seek a word from the Lord, I came forward at top speed.

I joined the end of Pete's ministry line, you can just imagine the scene,

When my turn came Pete laid hands on me and said: 'Ere bro, ave you been?'

4. Monkeys, Snakes and Spiders – India

There are some things that really give me the creeps.... I am a wuss of the first order when it comes to rats and snakes. I really think heaven is enjoying my discomfort as I travel to Africa and India and am continually confronted by these monsters.

On one of my first visits to India we visited an old mission hospital that had been turned into a Christian Conference Centre. It was like a throwback to old black and white films where these high-ceilinged whitewashed buildings are portrayed. I think the beds came from the old hospital. Metal bunks whose springs had seen better days with mattresses that would probably be classed as vintage back in the UK. It was in Nasra Por high up in the mountains some 3 hours travel from Mumbai.

We were given our room which was quite spacious. We had hardly been there more than a few minutes when we heard a lot of shouting and commotion coming from the large space at the centre of the building around which the rooms were situated. There in the middle of this room was one of the leaders of the church standing over a large black snake with red zigzag markings down its back. He held a stick on its head as he declared his triumph over this beast that he had discovered in the room next door to Irene and me. I quietly asked the guy standing next to me whether this snake was poisonous. He replied, "Very poisonous". I asked, "What does that mean?" and he declared that you would be dead in about 30 minutes if bitten by said reptile. I asked where the nearest hospital was. "About one hour away", he replied. My maths kicked into action as I realised if bitten by this animal you were unlikely to survive. It was an opportunity to put Mark 16 into action I surmised.

We searched our room, looking in every drawer and cupboard, under the bed and in the washroom. All we found was a friendly little frog in the damp toilet area. He remained with us for the week. We did have a visit from several rats who fortunately did not stay around.

We held meetings in a well-ventilated room, which had no windows and allowed a breeze to blow through the place. As we left one meeting, I noticed a large spider's web about 2 metres in diameter. It went from the guttering on the roof of the building right across one of the windows and was attached to small fence nearby. In the centre of the web was a large spider with a round, bright yellow body approximately 2 centimetres in size. Its legs were about 4 centimetres long. Again, I enquired of one of the guys walking with us about the danger this spider was to us. He declared the brighter the colour of the spider the more poisonous and dangerous it was. Seeing the strength of the colour of the beast I found myself asking how long you might have if bitten by said insect. Again, the answer was about half an hour. Knowing the hospital was about 1 hour away I did not need to ask the obvious question. You realise how little we know of these matters here in the West.

The only animals that invaded us in this Conference Centre were the monkeys. There were these grey monkeys which were about 150 centimetres in size. They moved around in packs and sometimes entered the building looking for food. The first time I visited I took with me a young man preparing for ministry. He proudly displayed his new denim jeans. Levi 501's had just been launched and he wore his with pride. He told us how he had paid some £50 for these trousers. At that time that was a small fortune. After a few days they had become grubby and so he washed them carefully by hand. Just on the outskirts of the Centre grounds were some washing lines put up for those attending the place to dry their clothes. John took his jeans and carefully hung them on the clothesline. He had barely walked 10 metres away when from the forest nearby two or three of our monkey friends rushed to the line, extracted his jeans from the line and disappeared into the forest. His 501's never to be seen again. I must admit I did have a little chuckle to myself.

5. Rats in Kigali, Rwanda – Peter Butt

The first School of Ministries teaching in Rwanda was carried out by me accompanied by an excellent bible teacher from our local church. He was a very well-educated man and held an important post in the judicial system in the UK. He agreed to travel with me.

We were to travel to Kigali, the capital city of Rwanda and be accommodated in the Pastor's house which we were told had recently been built. What we were not told is that the house had been partiality built and although it was waterproof there were many fixtures and fittings that had not been put in place. I arrived from Kampala at the weekend and my friend was to join me on the Monday. I was introduced to our "visitors" on Sunday afternoon. I was sitting in the "lounge" on a rather scruffy sofa when I heard some scratching activity at the back of the chair. I asked what that was and was told it was our "visitors"; being rather naïve I asked who the visitors were, to be told it was the rats. This was the beginning of a nightmare for me. I hate rats! Over the next days I discovered the house was full of them. The walls for the rooms in the house had been built but no ceilings had yet been fixed. This meant that noise carried throughout the house. It also meant there were runways along the top of the walls for rats to travel at speed around the house. It was very disconcerting to lie in bed and see all these little, beady eyes peering down at you as you were trying to get to sleep. We were each given a mosquito net, but they had gaping holes in them so were not ideal. I imagined a rat descending on me in the middle of the night. Fortunately, it never happened.

One day while having breakfast a rat ran down the wall at the other side of the room, ran across the floor and up the other side of the wall. No one turned a hair. I was blubbering.... "Look at that". The leader and his wife had a couple of small children and one new-born. I suggested having rats in the house was not helpful in creating a good environment for them to be. Could they not do something about them. He replied that if you put rat poison down, the rat goes away and dies in some obscure place and fills the house with the most awful smell of decaying flesh. He suggested it is better to live in peaceful co-existence. For the whole week we did just that. My fellow traveller in an adjacent bedroom did have a visitor in the night who was scrabbling round the floor and then hid behind a wardrobe. After some commotion he managed to encourage the visitor to leave. He ran under the door and straight into my room and up the wall and away. We did not enjoy sufficient sleep that night.

At the end of the week the leader requested that School of Ministries return to complete more teaching. I tactfully, as I could, suggested that when we returned, we would need to stay in accommodation that was rat free as we were not used to these creatures and our lack of sleep affected our teaching capacity. He turned to my companion and said, "You don't feel like that do you?". In a wonderful, humble, and kind way he answered. "Well actually, I do".

On the last day in the house, I visited the bathroom for my morning wash and brush up and there on the tap was the most enormous grasshopper I had ever seen. I groaned. How could I turn the tap on with this monster in my way. Eventually I summed up the courage to encourage the beast to move and went about my ablutions watched by this monster locust. I have often laughed as I thought about the visitors we had encountered in that place.

We did return but found suitable accommodation that was rat-less!

6. Methodist Missionary Conference Centre Malindi – Peter Butt

Irene and I were teaching in Malindi, a city on the coast of Kenya. The students were situated in a Conference Centre, but we were told it was too basic for us. We were accommodated in a Methodist Conference Centre, which had only been open for one year and our friends who organised the trip assured us it was clean and well appointed, as they had stayed there the previous year. We arrived and immediately began to be a little concerned. There were just a couple of young guys who looked about 16 looking after the place. Eventually they found our booking and took us to our room. We walked into the room to see the "ensuite" bathroom on the left. There was a shower tray that looked as though it hadn't been cleaned for a year, no curtain, and where the rose should be there was an open pipe. I asked about hot water and was told only cold water was provided. We looked at the toilet. There was no seat or fittings, it was just the bowl, again it didn't look as if it had been cleaned. The sink had rusty fittings and the water dribbled from the tap. Hardly a good start.

The room was a reasonable size but there was no furniture or even a chair, just the bed. We were relieved to see a fan on the ceiling. It was also a surprise to see that in place of windows there was a netting covering the window space. The bedding was very worn and scruffy and there was what looked like flock blankets from the second world war covering the mattress. Irene was not happy.... But there was nothing we could do.

By evening we had made ourselves as comfortable as possible and settled down to sleep. The young guys were seated outside under a veranda where there was a television blaring out the latest African music. As there were no windows, we "enjoyed" the full blast of this musical interlude. We tried to sleep but found it very difficult. Fortunately, the ceiling fan worked. However, when it had been fitted it was placed too close to the wall so every time the fan went round it clonked against the wall and was so loud that it was impossible to sleep. We switched the fan off. The music stopped and so we felt at last we would be able to sleep. After some minutes I felt something on my feet. I pulled the covers back and switched on the light, my feet were crawling with red ants, absolutely covered in them. That was the last straw that broke the camel's back. We got through the night and the next day expressed our displeasure at the service and moved to a local hotel run by some German folk. Joy! We had a brilliant time for the rest of the week.

7. House of Horrors in Australia – Peter Butt

Not every difficult domestic situation we have experienced was in the developing nations. We also had a rather interesting time in a house in Australia. We were ministering in a Bible School in Sydney and were accommodated in the house of a businessman. He was extremely well off and as he drove us to his house advised us that the large, riverside property he had acquired had won a prize for its unusual architecture. We looked forward with great expectation and when we saw the place we were not disappointed. Built into a cliff side, leading down to a river this magnificent glass building on 4 or 5 floors looked stunning.

However, when we entered the building, our delight turned to surprise which led to stunned silence as we experienced the totally impractical nature of this glass house.

It was suspended on 4 massive poles, larger than the telegraph poles used in the UK. A central suspended metal staircase comprising of a short series of stairs at right angles, ran down the centre of the property. Out from these stairs at each mezzanine floor various rooms were suspended. A wooden floor in a metal frame was encased by glass from floor to ceiling. Blinds were placed at each of these glass walls. You entered at the cliff top, which was level with the road and descended, there was a bedroom on the right, then stairs, then the lounge, a few more stairs and the kitchen appeared, a few more and it was the dining area, then down to the bedrooms and bathrooms. There were no doors on the rooms, just short passageways. The only room with a door was the bathroom.

Eventually we were taken down to the bottom floor of the house and shown our bedroom, it was then Irene exclaimed where is the door. I suggested we did not need one as we were at th bottom of the house and in the passageway on our left there was a bathroom with a door that we thought was for our exclusive use. We proceeded to settle in, after all it was our home for a week. We then undressed and having put on our nightwear made our way into the bed. We had barely pulled up the covers before the son of the householder, in his late teens, came bounding down the stairs and entered the bathroom some two metres from our bed. He waved and greeted us as he entered the room. I looked at Irene, shocked and aware that just a few minutes earlier we had been naked as we prepared for bed. We were relieved he had not made the journey a short while before.

We slept reasonably well but were awakened in the morning. The whole room was shaking, I wondered if an earthquake was about to break out. We lay in bed looking at one another, totally confused. After a few seconds, Irene began to laugh and said, "It is the washing machine finishing its cycle with a fast spin. We then realised that the whole thing was suspended, and every movement caused the whole building to bounce. We then experienced a heavy rainfall and discovered that the bouncing had caused water leaks in the glass walls where the sealant had been affected. Every time it rained, we had to make sure our belongings were not anywhere near the walls.

The businessman and his wife had not been Christians very long and his son had not yet committed his life to Jesus. His young lady lived with them, and they both had separate bedrooms. As I previously mentioned there were no doors to any of the rooms. The young guy had the room or rather space immediately to the right of the front entrance. It did not have walls but rather a balcony about a metre high overlooking the lounge. One time, Irene and I arrived back at the house and let ourselves in; it was mid-afternoon. As we entered the house our eyes were drawn to the bedroom/space on the right where the guy and his girlfriend were engaged in some hanky-panky. He waved at us as we entered and said, "Hi". Embarrassed, we returned his greeting and made our way to our bedroom where we remained until we heard the owners return to the house.

Our hosts were very kind and looked after us extremely well, but we were not sorry to leave behind this prize winning house of horrors.

8. Culture and eating – Peter Butt

As a child the often-pronounced quote was, "Cleanliness is next to Godliness". There is definitely no Bible precedent for this statement, and it seemed to include within it a whole series of behaviours including table protocol, and the correct use of the knife and fork which were seen as essential elements of the classic Christian family. We were taught to hold the knife and fork properly, to use the back of our fork for collecting the food. This was alright except when peas were on the menu. Chasing your peas round the plate and either stabbing them or squashing them on the back of the fork was an acquired art. Putting your elbows on the table was another unchristian act. Good manners were seen as part of the Christian heritage expressed in the eating behaviour of the family.

It was then quite a shock to visit the USA for the first time. Seeing leaders of churches decimate their dinner by sawing up the food first with the knife and then putting down the knife and using their fork as a shovel. This was beyond belief for the respectable, English, Christian leader. After realising that I couldn't find a Bible verse to correct my errant friends I began to wonder if it was alright to use my fork as a shovel. In fact, you could pick up far more peas in this way and a thunderbolt from heaven did not strike me to the ground when I tried it out.

The situation did not improve when I first visited Asia. In India I found that many, if not most of the people used their fingers to eat. There were always bowls of water to wash your hands first, but this was taking things a little too far. However, there were times when I found myself happily eating food without any utensils and surprisingly enjoying the experience. It was not long before I began to prefer using my fingers to eat whenever I could. Somehow it tasted better and seemed a more authentic way of eating. My prayer life didn't suffer, and I found myself identifying with the people and their culture in a deeper way.

Now I enjoy eating spareribs with my fingers, and I watch with amusement as my friends try to dissect them with a knife and fork.

Anyway, we Brits have long ago discovered the pleasure of eating with our fingers. Fish and Chips to take away, wrapped in paper, doused in salt and vinegar, eaten walking along the promenade at the sea front. We have always known the joy of such indulgence and we are still Christians!

9. First Mission trip to Kenya - Peter Butt

My first missions' trip to Kenya was in the early 90's and I accompanied my friend Simon Newberry who had made a number of connections in this great country.

We arrived in Nairobi and stopped over for one night. A young man met us and took us to our accommodation. Simon in those days delighted in finding ridiculously cheap guest houses. They were not only low on cost but on everything else as well. A meeting was held in a small open room with no windows. A single light was strategically placed over the hastily acquired lectern. As I preached, an enormous moth the size of a bat intruded in our gathering attracted by the light. It interfered with my preaching. Exasperated I took a swipe at the monster and completely missed it but smashed the only light bulb we had into a million pieces. Candles were lit but I hobbled through the rest of my message under severe restrictions. Not a particularly grand start to my mission into Kenya.

We made our way by road to Kisumu. It took over 5 hours. We endured several punctures and other obstacles on the road which in those days, was in places almost impassable. We then discovered you could fly in 30 minutes for a very reasonable price which became our future mode of travel.

Again, Simon had acquired cheap guest house accommodation in Kisumu. The room in which we were situated was simple, very simple. Just two beds and a sink. Unfortunately, the water authority had not paid the electricity bill, so the water had been cut off. It meant there was no water being pumped into the system. In this stifling atmosphere, with no relief from the heat and no water to cool us down we tried to sleep. The bed was ancient, it had springs that sank in the middle and creaked every time you moved. The mattress was only a couple of inches deep. I could not sleep; I was so hot. Eventually I took the mattress and placed it on the floor directly below the window where there was a slight breeze. I enjoyed some relief until from the heavens something dropped on my bare chest, scurried across my body and disappeared into the mist. I have no idea whether it was a gecko, a spider or a rat, but it frightened the life out of me. The next day I suggested to Simon we required better accommodation. We managed to find a much more satisfactory place for our stay.

On another day we were to visit a village outside of Kisumu called Kijulu. A meeting was arranged and the village elders from the villages in the district had been invited to a mid-day meal to meet with us. I had no idea of the culture or protocols but had the presence of mind to take with me the obligatory toilet paper. A meal of generous proportions was provided and every time my place was cleared more food was added. I enjoyed the meal, but it was a little spicy. We talked and ate under a tree in the centre of the village as was the custom.

After a while the food I had eaten began to work in my digestion system and I became increasingly aware that I required the use of the toilet facilities. I managed to quietly ask the whereabouts of the bathroom to be pointed to a square wooden shack about 10 metres away set up on a raised area of ground. I think the Aussies call it "a dunny". I made my way to said building and opened the door to be met by a multitude of flies and other insects. I was completely uninitiated to the practice of crouching over a small slot in a concrete slab, this was placed over a "long drop" a 2 metre by 1 metre hole dug in the ground.

I placed my toilet paper along the edges of this 30cm by 10cm slot and took my place, crouching was out of the question. As I relaxed, I experienced an enormous release of wind. It sounded like a volcano and was amplified by the echo in the long drop. A 15cm green and red lizard shot out of the hole between my legs and directly in front of me. I had obviously frightened the poor animal to death. Unfortunately, his sudden and unexpected movement had the same effect on me, and I fell backwards, my feet in the air, opening the door of the shed and revealing myself in all my glory to a startled audience of village elders from the area. It was like something from a Charlie Chaplin film.

I learned so much from my first visit to Kenya and rural Africa which has stood me in good stead for my further visits over the years.

10. Culture – Peter Butt

One of the other interesting features of travelling abroad is to encounter the different cultures. It is an interesting often intriguing experience. Culture is valid and Paul in the book of Romans validates culture when he mentioned we should give "custom to whom custom is due"; he acknowledges there are different responses and behaviours in different nations. My understanding is that culture is good and identifies a people except where it impinges on Kingdom principles as expressed in the scripture and then it is culture that must change.

I have mentioned our first excursion to Rwanda. I travelled with an excellent man of character who exercised a very responsible position in our British judicial process. During his excellent teaching on the character of the leader, he mentioned that every morning his first task was to take his wife a cup of tea in bed around 6.30am in the morning. The 70 African leaders burst into laughter believing this was a joke. My friend looked round at me nonplussed by this response. I said to him, "They do not believe you; they think you are joking, explain to them this is what you really do? He emphasised this again and once more the response was laughter probably even louder than before. I stood to my feet and carefully and slowly explained that he did this as an act of love expressing a servant heart. They eventually got the message and were absolutely floored by the thought that they might make a cup of tea for their wives; after all, that was her responsibility. It was a revealing moment for both them and us.

Another time in Kenya we had been teaching on marriage over several years and encouraging the African men to show affection and regard to their wives. We discovered later that they had dismissed most of our teaching as "white men's" interpretation of the Bible. That is until I took a West Indian brother and his wife who had been in the UK for many years. He taught the same thing and then expressed his love and regard for his wife by honouring her, walking alongside her, holding her hand as they walked along. All these were actions foreign to our friends in Africa. Several of the leaders came to us following the teaching and acknowledged they had not listened to us before but now saw that they needed to give attention to these matters. It was a joy to see them embracing some of these relationship enhancing activities as we returned to that city over the next few years.

Another situation arose in South Africa that was very revealing to us which enabled us to address another issue where culture required refining. We were talking about family and discovered that in the rural areas it was an accepted practice for men to father children outside of marriage and for the girl's father to take on responsibility for the child. When we discovered this, we taught on the responsibility of being a father, that although this might be the cultural practice, they still had responsibility. It was quite amusing to see many of the men of all ages squirm as we realised, they had adapted this practice before they were married and before they took up leadership in the church. They tried to come up with arguments that would let them off the hook. However, the Holy Spirit helped us, and we had an excellent time of ministry as they acknowledged their need to take on the children they had produced.

There are so many stories about culture as is seen in other anecdotes in this book. It is part of the joy of travelling to uncover healthy cultural practices and challenging them when culture requires some adjustment to bring them into line with Kingdom values.

11. Culinary Delights in Pakistan – Paul Randerson

I was travelling in Northern Pakistan around the city of Peshawar. An American guy with a prophetic ministry was working with me. On one occasion we were invited to preach the gospel and pray for the sick in an extremely poor catholic area called "Father Colony". After some great meetings we were invited to eat a kind of rice and vegetable dish with nan bread. We ate in a dingy courtyard, as we sat to eat our meal, I could not really see what I was eating but I was so hungry I wolfed it down.

My American friend said, "Did you look at your rice before you ate it?" "No" I answered, "Why?" He passed me his plate and I could see the rice was moving! I have no idea what it was in the rice I dashed into the road and threw up the meal I had just eaten. I decided fasting was a good idea when we went into these areas.

5

Problems in the Pulpit

1. Be prepared – Ken Ford

From the ages of 7 to about 18 my life was dominated by the scout movement – I was part of a brilliant troop and had many wonderful experiences, including trips overseas. The motto of the scouts was 'Be prepared' and in general it has stood me in good stead, though not necessarily in the realm of overseas ministry trips.

In another entry in this volume, I've mentioned my visit to Renggam in Malaysia – in fact I think it was my first ever overseas jaunt. A large group of us, mostly from New Zealand, gathered at a hotel in Singapore where we prayed and prophesied over each other before setting off in groups to cross the border into Malaysia. I seem to remember I was in a minibus with three others, and it was clear we were to be taken to four separate locations. Each of us in turn was summoned to the front seat where we were told where we were being taken and what was required of us while we were there.

I listened as the other three were given their instructions, and then my turn came. I was full of expectation and excitement, until the driver announced: 'Pastor Ken Ford, you will go to Renggam where you will preach for three nights on Second coming of Lord Jesus Christ.' Now some of you reading this will regard this as a brilliant opportunity but I must be honest and tell you that my heart sank.

I had two bags with me – a small one containing a change of underwear and a toothbrush, and a much larger one containing all my accumulated sermon notes and teaching material gleaned over many years of ministry. I had notes on every subject under the sun... except... the Second coming of the Lord Jesus Christ!

I'm aware of the various positions people take on the second coming – Premillennialist, (the millennial will come after the return of Jesus), Post millennialist (millennial before the return of Jesus} and A-millennialist (no literal millennium.) I hope you won't be too shocked to know that I'm a Pan millennialist – I'm not sure what to think but I know it will all pan out in the end! So, imagine my consternation at the thought that for three sessions I was to teach on a subject I was so unsure about. I prayed with some desperation, and a moment of revelation came.

I had become a Christian through connecting with the Navigators, and excellent organisation working in universities and colleges. Part of their discipleship package was TMS, the Topical Memory System, whereby we learnt key passages from the Bible, including ensuring that we knew the reference as well as the actual verse. For example, Philippians 4:13 'I can do all things through Christ who gives me strength' Philippians 4:13 – we had to say the refence before and after. As a result, I know quite a lot of Bible verses and quite a few references – increasingly my challenge is that I can't always remember which reference goes with which verse!

Anyway, into my mind came Hebrews 10:25 – 'Let us not give up meeting together as some are in the habit of doing. Instead let us encourage one another, and all the more so as you see the Day approaching.' Why has the word 'Day' got a capital letter? It's because it refers to the day of 'Second coming of Lord Jesus Christ!' Yes, Yes, Yes!

So, for three nights I shared on how we prepare for 'Second coming of Lord Jesus Christ' through the different ways in which we can encourage one another – fellowship, prayer, prophecy, hospitality and so on. I was able to move on, secure in the knowledge that I was leaving a church who may have been a little unsure about 'Second coming of Lord Jesus Christ,' but boy, did they know how to encourage one another!

2. Most Embarrassing Preach Ever – Peter Butt

Most preachers can tell amusing stories of communication mistakes. Some were insignificant and others causing reactions of laughter or even irritation or anger. I have completed my share of such indiscretions but by far the worst was at one of our youth camps in the mid-80's.

I was preaching on how special and significant every individual is to God. Chosen, called, and set apart for God. There were some 200 in the congregation mainly between 13 and 25 years old plus leaders and staff.

I was well into my message when I came to a place in my notes where I read. "Tony Campolo illustration". I heard this brilliant communicator just a few months before describing how everyone is special, he suggested everyone is a winner. He described the process of conception, that many sperms were in a race to activate the seed, but you were the one who had made it ahead of many others. I had not thought through how I would present this sensitive illustration or considered that I was speaking to young people.

As I began, I was aware of this and found myself searching for the right words. I started with wanting to mention there were millions of sperm waiting in the scrotum. Thinking on my feet I realised it would be difficult to use the correct words. So I started with the words, "There you were like millions of...... tadpoles in a ..... reservoir waiting for the race to start". I was really struggling, looking for the right means of communication. (In the mid-80's there were various words for the act of intercourse, one of which was "bang", I believe it still is used in some contexts as a description of this activity.)

I then said with great enthusiasm, totally unaware of the connection, "Then suddenly Bang, the race started". There was a stunned silence for several seconds after which the whole crowd from the youngest to the eldest began to howl with laughter. My fellow minister for that week was a friend of mine, Mike Godward. He had a propensity to laugh very loudly and wholeheartedly. He fell from his seat and was laying on the platform with his feet in the air convulsed with laughter. I realised my terrible mistake and began to laugh along with everyone else. I looked across the rows of laughing youngsters and saw there were only 3 teenagers not laughing but looking shocked and surprised. They were my 3 teenage daughters who could not believe what I had said.

After what seemed an age, the giggling began to subside, and I thought to myself I have to get this back to some semblance of order. I prepared my next sentence determined to speak with force and authority to bring things back into line. I prepared to say, "Yes there you were one in a million and you made it, you are a winner". I was so taken up with ensuring I brought some decorum to the meeting that I over emphasised my speech. I said, "Yes there you were one in a *willion*".

If the previous gaff had brought laughter this one brought the house down. I completely lost it. It was probably 15 or 20 minutes before we could continue. Any anointing there had been had completely disappeared, any effect I hoped to achieve was lost and that was that. It is the only time in over 50 years of preaching that such a disaster occurred. Thankfully.

6

Prayer and Prophecy Bloopers

Some interesting prayers have been prayed in local church gatherings; alongside over enthusiastic prophecies that have also caused some amusement. I am sure those who were praying and prophesying had no idea of the unintended other meaning of their sincere intercession.

1. Whoops - Ian Jennings

In South Wales an elderly member of the church eloquently said in the prayer meeting. "Dear Lord please forgive us for our falling shorts!"

In a church in the midlands in a local church prayer meeting, an elderly member of the church prayed. "Please bless sister Brenda with healing; you know Lord that she is 84...' There was a sudden interruption from the lady sitting next to her, "No she isn't, she's 83." "Oh no she isn't," replied the prayer. "Yes, she is," insisted the other. The lady on her feet praying said, "Look I should know, I've known her since we were girls together." Then unabashed carried on ... 'so Lord you know she is 84 and getting a bit frail ...'

2. Prayer for Provision – Peter Butt

A local church was struggling financially, a special prayer meeting was called. The up-to-date situation was shared before the people began to pray. An older lady in the congregation had recently come to faith and was enthusiastically enjoying her newfound relationship with God. I guess in her memory somewhere she had heard the name of God, "Jehovah Jireh – The Lord will provide". She prayed with great gusto and as she came to the conclusion of her prayer she said, "We know you will meet this need because you are Jehovah Giro". (For those who are younger or whose memory is not so good, when the government paid benefits they used the Post Office to dispense cheques which were called Giros')

3. Does God speak like this? – Ian Jennings

In a local church in West Yorkshire an intense, over-enthusiastic young man trying his hand at prophecy said, "Thus saith the Lord, 'I've had a belly full of you lot, you'd better pull your socks up or else!!'"

4. Prophesy of approval – Peter Butt

In a local church Sunday meeting in Kent, following a very successful Saturday where the church had enjoyed a BBQ and a Barn Dance, a prophecy was given which started with the words, "Thus says the Lord.... I have not enjoyed myself so much since the marriage of Cana".

5. Unusual prayers – Peter Butt

In my first church a lady prayed the following prayer, "Lord please bless Mrs Richards, I have had her leg on my heart all night".

As a young man I remember some awful prayer meetings in the local church. One guy prayed every week for about 20 minutes. He prayed for everybody and everything in a boring, monotone voice. The one highlight that we listened for every week was when he prayed for the missionaries. At that time Donald and Eunice Crook were in

India and Fred and Mary Ramsbottom were in Congo. Without any change in his intonation, he would pray for the "crooks in India" and the "rams bottoms in Congo". I often wondered what anyone coming into the meeting who did not have the full picture made of those prayers!

6. Prayer Meetings – Roger Blackmore

In the early 70's there was a man in our church who would passionately pray for missionaries on a regular basis, but he didn't always get it right.

Like the time he petitioned God at great length for "all the missionaries throughout the whole universe" and got me wondering which planets were now being evangelized.

On another occasion. I guess he intended to use the word "secular" but as he spoke the words, what came out was. "We pray for our missionaries, who have given up their *sexual* lives"!

I wonder if the world record for long prayers might have been the objective of a dear old member of our church in Scotland years ago. On our monthly Day Of Prayer, the church was open all day for people to come in and pray for a while. There were seldom more than a handful there at any one time, but I stayed throughout. At one point it was just Robert and myself and for some reason, as he started to pray aloud, I glanced at my watch. I did the same, but totally intentionally, when he finally finished his prayer with the words, "But Lord, what can we say to you?" He had been at it for over 25 minutes, and I mischievously thought, "For someone who doesn't know what to say to God, you've been doing pretty well at it." God forgive me!

I'll never forget the morning I nearly spat out the contents of the communion cup all over the usher who had just handed it to me. I was pastoring a church that celebrated communion every Sunday morning, with three trays of broken crackers, one for each section of seats, and three silver goblets filled with grape juice. The dreaded "common cup" had been the pattern for years and it was passed from worshipper to worshipper along with a napkin, so that you could wipe off the remains of the saliva of whoever may have ended up sitting next to you. On this particular day, the contents of the goblets looked much lighter than usual as I prayed over them and handed them to the ushers for distribution. As was the pattern, one of these men then passed a cup back to me and I took a sip from it first.

Whatever it was tasted revolting, and it was all I could do not to grimace, let alone not to spit it out. I had no idea what this vile concoction was, but I must admit that I took a morbid pleasure in watching the reactions of the congregation as the evil brew was shared. It turned out that the dear lady who prepared communion faithfully every week had arrived early that day only to discover there was none of the grape juice that she regularly used. Panicking, she looked around the kitchen for alternatives and the best she could think of was cans of Dr. Pepper that were in the fridge. Realizing a carbonated drink might not be a great choice, she poured sugar into the Doctor Pepper and then added some cold water. And that was how an avid Diet Coke fan was almost poisoned by a cocktail made from a drink I detest to start with.

7

Miscellaneous

1. Songs I cannot sing

There are some great songs that I can no longer sing. An unfortunate experience, usually related to an innocent mistake in the use of the words has meant I find it very difficult to sing without my memory kicking in with an "alternative" version.

This all started when I was a boy. At Sunday School we learnt many songs, one I never understood properly as the words seemed at variance to the gospel that spoke of love and kindness. The words of Jesus were particularly important, and one song seemed in opposition to the message. We had a Scottish song leader, he led us with great enthusiasm; "I will make you vicious old men, vicious old men, vicious old men. I will make you vicious old men if you follow me". I sang along but was rather confused until several years later I became aware that the actual words of the song were "I will make you fishers of men if you follow me". A direct quote from the gospels. All became clear.

We then moved onto Christmas Carols. There were all the usual "revised versions" made up to amuse. Various versions of "While shepherds watched" or "We Three Kings" However, it was one of the later verses of that carol that caught my attention. The week before Christmas we would often go carol singing around the streets, I remember standing next to a gentleman as we sang. He began to sing; "Thus spoke the Sheriff and forthwith appeared a shining throng". I was intrigued and had to take a double take to see that the words were "Thus spoke the Seraph". I cannot sing that verse without smiling!

As a boy the cutting-edge radio comedy show was called, "Beyond our Ken". It referred to the host of that show whose name was Kenneth Horne. Hymn 699 in the Redemption Hymnal was a beautiful, worship song about Jesus. Unfortunately, in the second verse we have the line, "Pouring out love beyond our Ken". The writer was using a Scottish word that meant beyond our understanding or knowledge. However, every time I sang it, excerpts from the comedy, radio show flashed into my memory and spoilt the devotional nature of the song. It was also a means of a moment of unintended amusement in a funeral service. A friend who we had met at Bible College had passed away and three of us who had been at college with him attended the gathering. The name of the guy was Ken. Imagine our surprise when we sang this hymn. I struggled to suppress my laughter and dared not look at my friends who I could see were in the same state as we sang the second verse.. Fortunately, no one else in the gathering was as unspiritual as us!

It was round the dinner table on a Sunday that the next song was spoiled for me. My youngest daughter suddenly piped up and said, "What's that song about dear pants". We looked up taken back by the question and did not immediately have an answer. My wife was the first to fall in and said, "You mean, "As the deer pants for the water so my soul longs after you". Another great song ruined for me.

One more.... There was a lively song that brought joy to congregations as they reflected on the wonder of this glorious salvation. It went. "I get so excited Lord every time I realise, I'm forgiven, I'm forgiven." Then at various places in the song the words are repeated, "I'm forgiven, I'm forgiven". However, once someone indicated to me that some young boys had been singing, "I'm a gibbon", instead of I'm forgiven" another song was lost to me.

There are more but these are the main examples. Am I the only unspiritual one?

2. Salvation at Camp – Peter Butt

For some 15 years in the 70's and 80's Irene and I led youth camps in Great Walstead School, Lindfield, Sussex. These were exciting times when many young people from across the nation experienced encounters with God that transformed their lives. Even now some 40 years later stories emerge of those touched by God during those days. A number of those who attended those camps are in church leadership in this nation and abroad. We also had some unusual times which we look back at with gratitude to God for how He saved us from disaster and trouble.

On one of those occasions, I awoke early in the morning to a sound of a thunderous roar. To describe it is difficult. It reminded me of an old-fashioned steam roller or a massive cement mixer. The sound was overwhelming. I had no idea what it was. I left my bed and the room where I was sleeping and sought out the guy who that week was responsible for maintenance. I woke him up and requested he come with me to explore where this massive explosive sound was coming from. His background was as an electrician, and he had been involved in the building trade all his working life. He could not explain this noise.

We began to investigate and discovered the sound was coming from the basement. As we arrived closer to the sound, we realised it was in the boiler room. The school had an extremely large gas boiler providing water and heating to the whole building. As we opened the door the sound increased yet again; it was deafening, and we had to shout to make ourselves heard.

It is fascinating how people react differently in a crisis. I was standing still, rooted to the spot thinking things through. I was as cool as a cucumber. My thoughts were that we needed to deal with this, or we could be blown to smithereens in an instant. My colleague reacted more actively, he started running backwards and forwards across the room shouting, "What shall we do, we will all be blown up." it reminded me of the famous "Jonesy" in the TV series Dads Army who often reacted in the same way saying, "Don't panic, don't panic" when he was absolutely stricken with fear. After what seemed like an eternity but was probably just a few seconds I suggested there might be a master switch that could shut the whole thing down. I managed to penetrate the thinking of my partner and he went to the far end of the room and pulled down a large red lever which instantly shut the whole thing off. We breathed a sigh of relief. The only casualty was that the campers had to wash in cold water that morning! Later that day the gas repair guy turned up and discovered that the pilot light had gone out and that gas was still pumping through, hence the thunderous sound. He did suggest that the whole place could have blown up if a spark had ignited the gas that filled the room. It is amusing to recount the story; it was quite a different story to be in that room at the time of the event. We give thanks to God for His deliverance!

On another occasion Irene experienced another evidence of the grace of God in the kitchen. There was a massive gas boiler used for heating water or boiling potatoes or even broiling chickens. It was in regular use and kept going during the day. One particular day Irene felt she should find some stones, wash them and place them at the bottom of the boiler. Her final job in the evening was to turn the gas off during the night. The next day we took a day off and enjoyed a break from the arduous work of running the camp. Instructions were left with the kitchen staff for the day. The following morning Irene was the first to enter the kitchen. The windows were running with water, the place was full of steam, the boiler was still alight, it had not been turned off the night before. She immediately rectified the situation and turned off the boiler. When she looked inside the boiler it was completely dry. The many gallons of water stored in the boiler had completely evaporated. The stones she has placed in the boiler had taken the heat and broken into many pieces the temperature having become that excessive. Again, we were saved from a major catastrophe. Later in the day we were advised that the stones had certainly saved us from a massive explosion which might well have caused damage to the building as well as the kitchen. We recognise the goodness of God in these stories alongside the smile they bring to us as we remember these events.

3. Be careful where you stand – Ken Ford

I was in Bangkok with my buddy Pete Light whose caring nature you can read about elsewhere. We were staying with our friends Phil and Cathy who were looking after us really well. They lived in a gated apartment block with a walled enclosure and a gate out onto a busy street. On our second day there, Cathy went off with Pete to pick up their car, and I was instructed to wait just outside the gate on the pavement.

It was quite early on a pleasant day and people were obviously making their way to work. A young woman approached and stopped opposite where I was standing. She turned to face me, placed her hands together in a prayerful pose and gently bowed.

I was aware of the high levels of respect and politeness exhibited by the Thai nation, but it was still a bit of a surprise. Naturally, wanting to identify with those I was among I dutifully placed my hands together, smiled and bowed in return. She returned my smile and walked on. I stood for a moment quite overwhelmed by the honour and respect I had experienced.

Moments later a group of three approached and exactly the same scenario repeated itself – all three prayerfully bowed. I was getting into the swing now, so I clasped hands and bowed to each one in turn before they moved on.

It was a heartwarming experience, but I found it a bit daunting as I looked to see quite a large number of people approaching and all seemed determined to greet me in the appropriate traditional manner. At a conservative estimate I would say at least forty people of all ages greeted me. Fortunately, Cathy and Pete arrived with the car and I climbed in.

'That was amazing' I announced, and in great detail told them of the remarkable level of warmth, welcome and honour I had experienced. I droned on about what a contrast it was to the British nod and 'Morning' you got back home if you were lucky. I felt it would be a treasured moment I would remember with great affection for the rest of my life.

When I eventually stopped, there was moments pause and Cathy said 'Ken, you were standing next to a shrine.'

4. Called to be a Missionary – Peter Butt

Following a Sunday morning service where the children had been privileged to hear a lady speaking about her mission's work in Africa, we arrived home. As usual my wife and I made our way to the kitchen to prepare dinner. It wasn't long before our middle daughter came into the kitchen and said she had been very impressed by the missionary lady and thought that she would like to be a missionary. We encouraged her, although only a child, that it would be a fine thing to do with her life. She left the room and we continued to prepare our Sunday roast. (Remember those!)

Several minutes later she arrived back with us with a question. "Do missionaries get eaten by cannibals?", she asked. We knew the source of this information. She had obviously been speaking with our youngest daughter who would suggest such a thing. We had to tell the truth. "Not usually", we replied. "Although it has been known that missionaries have lost their lives in this way". She once more left the room. We laughed as we knew the source of this question but wanted to treat her "call" seriously. It was several minutes later that she returned yet again. This time to declare, "I don't think I will be a missionary". I guess it might make the Guiness book of records for the shortest missions call ever!

5. Praying for the Sick – John Noble

Soon after I was baptised in the Holy Spirit as a young Christian, I was desperately keen to pray for the sick at every opportunity. One family welcomed me into their home to pray for their aged mother who was frail and quite ill. I was obviously very happy to do this and asked if they had some olive oil which I felt was a necessity in such circumstances. Sadly, they had no olive oil but had some Mazola cooking oil which I conceded was most likely an acceptable substitute to the Holy Spirit.

I had seen some Pentecostal ministers praying for the sick so I knew exactly what to do although I didn't realise how quickly cooking oil pours out of a Mazola bottle and my old lady got well and truly anointed! Undaunted, I began to shout just like my Pentecostal friends did, commanding the sickness to depart in the name of Jesus. After some time, I explained that healing often happens sometime after prayer and quietly took my leave.

It was a few days later that I heard the old lady had 'slipped' away to be with Jesus, no doubt the Mazola helped in the 'slipping' process. Undeterred, I have to confess that I found two more old ladies to pray for with very similar results, at least I was assured that they were lovely Christian old ladies so, thankfully, we knew where they went!

Following these experiences, I came to the conclusion that I had a ministry which the Catholics call the ' ministry of the last rites. Strangely, when I tell my story and offer to pray for anyone who is ready to receive their eternal reward no one has ever come forward yet.

6. What's in a name! – Ian Jennings

In the UK there are 3 main Pentecostal church streams. The Elim, Assemblies of God and Apostolic Church. In Aberaman, South Wales there was the Assemblies Of God which was called the Pentecostal Church and there was the Apostolic church which of course was called Apostolic Pentecostal Church. One guy came to us in the morning and the Apostolic church for the evening service. He had to go into hospital and when asked his religion he said, 'Apercostal Pentestolic!' It sounds more like a serious physical condition than a Christian church!

That's all folks! I do trust these stories have made you laugh.

A wise man once said, "Being cheerful keeps you healthy. It is slow death to be gloomy all the time." Proverbs 17:22 (GNB).

About The Author

Peter Butt trained in the Assemblies of God Bible College. Since 1970 he has been involved in church leadership.

Having founded and established the School of Ministries leadership training programme, he travelled widely nationally and internationally training leaders as well as overseeing churches in the UK.

He is married to Irene and has four children, seven grandchildren, and four great grandchild.

Other Books by Peter Butt

I f you have enjoyed this book, you may enjoy other books by Peter Butt.

The Pentecost Released Series

Pentecost Now... Pentecost Then... :

Despite there being many books on how to be filled with the Holy Spirit, this one is different...

The Holy Spirit has not been forgotten, He is still God. He is alive, active and moving in power today as He was in the days of the first outpouring on the disciples. In Pentecost Now, Pentecost Then, Peter Butt draws from over forty years experience teaching theology, preaching Christianity and ministering in the power of the Holy Spirit all over the world.

Join him as he shares his experiences and stories of miracles, all anchored in his deep love of God and rooted in sound, Biblical theology. Discover how you too can experience the liberation of the Holy Spirit, just as the early church did.

Follow this link to get your copy https://geni.us/pentecost1 or scan this QR code:

Pentecost Expressed

It's time to take a fresh look at the gifts of the Holy Spirit.

As The Holy Spirit continues to move, His Gifts are available to you. They are not reserved only for pastors and leaders. It's time to rediscover the amazing Gifts of the Holy Spirit for yourself. Discover how you can experience these gifts in a fresh and exciting way. Discover how you can use these gifts to spread the message of Jesus. The Holy Spirit is still using ordinary people to impact and transform the world. In Pentecost Expressed, Peter Butt draws from over forty years' experience teaching theology, preaching Christ and ministering on the power of the Holy Spirit all over the world.

Follow this link to get your copy https://geni.us/pentecost2 or scan this QR code:

Pentecost Released

Is it time for the accepted church leadership model to change?

Without banks, a river simply loses its impetus. So often a move or outpouring of the Holy Spirit has dissipated this way. Godly, biblical leadership, and the gifts of the Holy Spirit are prominent, strategic, and significant "banks" for the river that flows in the book of Acts. Peter's exploration of the fivefold ministry within a church leadership team is biblical, clear, and very compelling. Rich Robinson said: *"This is a valuable addition to the Fivefold / APEST and Leadership conversation..."*

Follow this link to get your copy https://geni.us/pentecost3 or scan this QR code:

Our Journey

Over 50 years Peter and Irene Butt have sought to follow Jesus in every part of their lives. They have experienced the incredible power of the Holy Spirit in the most extraordinary circumstances. The miraculous provision of God has come in the most unexpected ways.

These have all shaped their journey. This book tells the story of a man and his wife who have selflessly served God, making decisions that seemed contrary to what is normally expected.

Whatever stage in the journey you find yourself, this book will inspire and encourage you, as you to seek to walk with Jesus.

Follow this link to get your copy: https://geni.us/ourjourney or scan this QR code:

All these books are available on Amazon.

Printed in Great Britain
by Amazon

37369926R10067